Elon Musk

The Biography of the Billionaire Entrepreneur making the Future Fantastic; Owner of Tesla, SpaceX, and Twitter

By United Library

https://campsite.bio/unitedlibrary

G000075585

Introduction

Interested in learning about the life of one of the most influential entrepreneurs of our time?

Elon Musk is known for being a brilliant thinker and innovator. He has founded several successful businesses, including Tesla, SpaceX, and PayPal. In this biography book, you will learn about his life story and how he has become one of the most famous and respected businessmen in the world.

Elon Musk is a Renegade Billionaire Entrepreneur Who is Making the Future Fantastic. He is the founder of Tesla Motors, SpaceX, and also the owner of Twitter. He has also been described as the real-life Iron Man.

In this biography book, you will learn about his life and how he became one of the most innovative and successful entrepreneurs of our time. You will also learn about his vision for the future and how he is using his businesses to make it a reality. If you are interested in learning more about Elon Musk and his companies, then this biography book is for you.

This biography book is not only informative but also fascinating to read. It's a great way to learn more about one of the most inspiring entrepreneurs out there today. You will be inspired by his successes as well as his failures - which he has openly shared with the world.

Table of Contents

Introduction 2

Table of Contents.. 3

Elon Musk 5

Children, youth and training...................................... 8

Zip2 11

X.com, PayPal... 13

SpaceX... 16

Tesla 19

SolarCity.. 23

Tesla Energy... 24

Neuralink 25

OpenAI 26

The Boring Company 27

Method of work... 28

Hydrogen 29

Philanthropy 31

Awards and recognitions 34

Television 36

Interests 37

Policy... 38

Pressure groups 40

Religion 41

Cinema 43

Hyperloop 45

Music 47

Tributes on your products 48

Personal life 51

Controversies.. 53

SEC 55

The rescue in the Tham Luang cave 58

Joe Rogan.. 61

COVID-19 62

Dogecoin 63

Elon Musk

Elon Reeve Musk (Pretoria, June 28, 1971) is an American entrepreneur, investor and mogul of South African descent. He is the founder, CEO and chief engineer of SpaceX; angel investor, CEO and product architect of Tesla, Inc; founder of The Boring Company; and co-founder of Neuralink and OpenAI. With an estimated net worth of about $252 billion as of April 2022, Musk is the richest person in the world according to the Bloomberg Billionaires Index and the Forbes Real-Time Billionaires List.

Musk was born to a Canadian mother and a white South African father, and grew up in Pretoria, South Africa. He studied briefly at the University of Pretoria before moving to Canada at the age of 17. He enrolled at Queen's University and transferred to the University of Pennsylvania two years later, where he graduated in Economics and Physics. In 1995 he moved to California to attend Stanford University, but decided to pursue an entrepreneurial career instead, co-founding the web software company Zip2 with his brother Kimbal. The company was acquired by Compaq for $307 million in 1999. That same year, Musk co-founded online bank X.com, which merged with Confinity in 2000 to form PayPal. The company was bought by eBay in 2002 for $1.5 billion.

In 2002, Musk founded SpaceX, an aerospace manufacturer and space transportation services company, of which he is CEO and chief engineer. In 2004, he joined electric vehicle manufacturer Tesla Motors, Inc. (now Tesla, Inc.) as president and product architect, becoming its CEO in 2008. In 2006, he helped create SolarCity, a solar energy services company that was later acquired by Tesla and became Tesla Energy. In 2015, he co-founded

OpenAI, a non-profit research company promoting friendly artificial intelligence. In 2016, he co-founded Neuralink, a neurotechnology company focused on developing brain-computer interfaces, and founded The Boring Company, a tunneling company. He also agreed to buy US social network major Twitter in 2022 for $44 billion. Musk has also proposed the Hyperloop.

He has been criticized for making unscientific and controversial statements. In 2018, he was sued by the U.S. Securities and Exchange Commission (SEC) for falsely tweeting that he had raised financing for a private acquisition of Tesla. He settled with the SEC but did not admit guilt, temporarily resigning his chairmanship and agreeing to limitations on his use of Twitter. In 2019, he won a defamation lawsuit brought against him by a British spelunker who advised on the Tham Luang cave rescue. Musk has also been criticized for spreading misinformation about the COVID-19 pandemic and for his other views on issues such as artificial intelligence, cryptocurrencies and public transportation.

Children, youth and training

His parents, Errol Musk and Maye Haldeman, met in high school. He was a South African engineer and real estate developer who once co-owned an emerald mine in Zambia, near Lake Tanganyika. His mother is a nutritionist and model; originally from Canada, she moved to Pretoria in 1950.They married in 1970 and within three years had three children: Elon (June 28, 1971), Kimbal (September 20, 1972) and Tosca Musk (July 20, 1974). The family was very wealthy in Elon's youth; his father once said, "We had so much money that sometimes we couldn't even close our safe."

Elon Musk grew up in a large home with his siblings and several cousins. His mother worked at home as a nutritional consultant. On weekends she also worked as a model, so his children hardly saw their parents and had a lot of freedom to pursue their interests.

At the age of nine he began programming a Commodore VIC-20 that had 8 kilobytes of RAM. At the age of ten he learned to program. At twelve he designed his first program, a space game called Blastar, and sold it for the equivalent of $500 to the South African magazine *PC and Office Technology.* In 1984 they published the 167 lines of source code and reviewed "In this game you have to destroy an alien freighter carrying deadly hydrogen bombs and *Status Beam Machines.* The program makes good use of *sprites* and animations, and in this respect it is well worth reading."

The money he earned from programming was spent on comics, computers and role-playing games like *Dungeons and Dragons.*

In 1979, to escape the abuse of her husband, who used to beat her, Maye divorced and moved to Durban, where Errol challenged the divorce terms in court. Errol challenged the terms of the divorce in court. In 1981 Elon decided to move to Johannesburg with his father. Kimbal joined them four years later.

At school he had no friends and was mistreated by his classmates. After taking classes in karate, judo, wrestling and at the age of sixteen growing to 180 cm he began to defend himself. Aware that it would be easier to emigrate to the United States from Canada, he applied for a Canadian passport through his mother, who was born in Regina, Saskatchewan, of American parents. While waiting for documentation, he attended the University of Pretoria for five months; this allowed him to avoid compulsory military service in South Africa.

Since many of her relatives lived in Western Canada, in 1989 Elon, Kimbal and Tosca Musk, along with Maye Haldeman, moved to Kingston, Ontario. When she arrived, all of Maye's savings were locked up, so she had to work at various jobs.[*citation needed*] She rented a small apartment in Toronto where they spent three weeks removing staples from the floor and wallpaper from the walls. In the process, she cut her hand and put her modeling jobs at risk. With the first money she earned, Maye bought a thick rug so they could sleep on the floor of the apartment, and a computer for Elon. She then worked as a researcher at the University of Toronto and simultaneously taught nutrition and modeling classes two nights a week and also worked as a nutrition consultant and studied for her second dietetic master's degree. Her three children had to get scholarships, take out loans and work to go to university. Many times they could not eat red meat even once a week.

In 1992 Elon was awarded a scholarship to study economics and physics at the University of Pennsylvania.

He received his degrees in economics and physics from the Wharton School at the University of Pennsylvania. He then enrolled at Stanford to pursue his Ph.D., but after two days he dropped out to start his own company. In 1995 he intended to work for Netscape and went to their offices, but did not dare to talk to anyone out of shyness.

One of his professors at the University of Pennsylvania was CEO of a company in Los Gatos, Silicon Valley, researching electrolytic ultracapacitors for electric vehicles. Elon worked for a summer at Pinnacle Research. These ultracapacitors had a very high energy density, but their chemical components were expensive and sold by the milligram because there were very few mines to extract them and they were not scalable for mass production.

After earning his degrees, and inspired by innovators such as Nikola Tesla, he decided to go into three areas where he felt there were "major problems," as he would later point out: "One was the Internet, one was renewable energy, and one was space.

Zip2

Kimbal accompanied Elon on a car trip across the United States in one month, from Silicon Valley to Philadelphia, where Elon was to complete his studies at Penn. During the trip they talked a lot about starting a business. In 1995, Musk enrolled in the PhD program in Applied Physics and Materials Science at Stanford University, but within two days he dropped out of classes so he could found Zip2, along with his brother Kimbal Musk and his friend Greg Curry. Elon Musk was the CEO of Zip2. Zip2 managed the development, hosting and maintenance of websites specifically for media companies. This allowed them to establish a web presence through automatic editing by adding maps and route directions to go door-to-door to addresses (a business that anticipated what would become *Google Maps* combined with *Yelp*). To do this they got free use of Navteq mapping, which had cost $300 million. They applied the Java language to send the maps and directions as vector images instead of bitmaps, which were very slow to transmit over the fledgling Internet. Elon did the programming and engineering, while Kimbal did the sales and raised capital.

Elon was an immigrant on a temporary visa and Kimbal was an illegal immigrant in the U.S. Due to lack of financial resources Kimbal and Elon spent some time living in Zip2's 4m x 9m office and used the YMCA facilities for showers. They used to eat very cheaply at *Jack in the Box*. When they could afford it they moved into an apartment and Kimbal cooked for the entire Zip2 staff. His sister Tosca moved from Toronto to San Francisco and worked with them at Zip2.

As of February 1999, it managed nearly 200 Web sites, including the New York Today site, which was a local directory of *The New York Times*. Zip2 also managed parts of the Hearst Corporation, Times Mirror, Knight-Ridder and Pulitzer Publishing chains. Zip2 was sold to Compaq Computer in 1999 for $307 million, of which Elon received $22 million.

X.com, PayPal

In March 1999 Elon Musk, Ho, Harris Fricker and Christopher Payne founded X.com as a financial *startup.* Musk initially invested $12 million. Within five months of its founding Harris Fricker threatened that if he wasn't CEO he would leave with the rest to start another company. Elon Musk told him he should do it. Fricker, Ho and other key engineers left X.com. Fricker had a successful career as CEO of GMP Capital. Payne founded a private equity firm in Toronto.

X.com was one of the first internet banks. It had to fight numerous banking regulations. Its deposits were insured by the FDIC.

Confinity Inc. was a Silicon Valley software company founded in December 1998 by Max Levchin, Peter Thiel and Luke Nosek as a cryptographic company that processed electronic payments.In late 1999 Confinity launched its flagship product, PayPal, which through the infrared port allowed money to be sent between PDA users such as the Palm Pilot.

In March 2000 X.com and Confinity decided it made more sense to join forces than to waste money on advertising to attract the same customers. Combining the PayPal product with X.com's sophisticated services, they merged into a new entity called X.com of which Elon Musk was named CEO because he was the largest shareholder in the resulting merged company. Within weeks X.com raised $100 million in investment from Deutsche Bank and Goldman Sachs. At the time X.com had more than one million customers.

The two companies tried to bring their cultures together with little success. There were fights over the design of the company's technology infrastructure. The Confinity team, led by Levchin, wanted to use Linux open source software, while Musk wanted to use Microsoft's data center software.

X.com faced tough battles over technology infrastructure, online fraud and branding strategies. In September 2000, tensions within the management team escalated.

In January 2000 Elon Musk had married Justine Wilson. Work had not allowed them to go on a honeymoon. Nine months later they planned to combine business and leisure to take a trip to seek investment capital and end it with a honeymoon at the Sydney Olympics. At 10:30 p.m., when Musk was flying, an extraordinary meeting of X.com was held at which Elon Musk was removed as CEO and Peter Thiel was appointed. Elon Musk canceled his honeymoon, took the first plane back to California and asked the board to reconsider their decision.Musk eventually agreed to the reorganization and although his influence in the company decreased, Musk remained as a consultative advisor and continued to invest increasing his position as the largest shareholder.In June 2001 X.com changed its name to its PayPal product to PayPal Inc.

In 2002 PayPal went public. At that time the company was making $240 million a year with PayPal. When eBay showed interest in buying PayPal, most wanted to sell as soon as possible. Musk and Mortiz asked the board to reject the first offers. In July 2002 eBay raised the offer to $1.5 billion and the board and Musk accepted the sale.

In October 2002, eBay acquired PayPal for $1.5 billion in stock. Prior to the sale, Musk was the majority shareholder, holding 11.7% of PayPal shares.

With the sale Elon Musk earned $180M after taxes. He dedicated $100M to found SpaceX, $70M to Tesla, Inc. and $10M to SolarCity. Several PayPal team members founded their own companies, including YouTube (Chad Hurley, Steve Chen and Jawed Karim), LinkedIn (Reid Hoffman), Yelp (Russel Simmons, Jeremy Stoppelman), Palantir Technologies, and Jammer.

Others, such as Peter Thiel, Reid Hoffman and Botha, became major investors in the tech industry. In 2015 eBay spun off PayPal to make it an independent company.

SpaceX

In 2002, Elon Musk began investigating the feasibility of sending a vehicle to Mars. Each Delta-2 rocket cost $50 to $60 million per mission and at least two missions were needed. He made three trips to Russia and tried unsuccessfully to buy ICBM intercontinental rockets without the warheads. On the plane back with his partners Mike Griffin and Jim Cantrell, Elon showed them a spreadsheet he had been working on for months. It was the first SpaceX prototype where he detailed all the parts of the business. The design would use reusable rockets. It would have a vertical integration strategy. In customer needs there was an emerging niche for launching small satellites. It would analyze cost and profit criteria. The business model would be that of a private aerospace company. He had also studied the physics behind the rocket structure and launch.

In June 2002, Musk founded his third company, Space Exploration Technologies (SpaceX), of which he is currently chief executive officer and chief technology officer. SpaceX is dedicated to developing and producing space shuttles, with an emphasis on cost reduction and high reliability. The first two transport rockets developed by SpaceX are the Falcon 1 and Falcon 9, and its first capsule is the Dragon.

On December 23, 2008 SpaceX signed a $1600 million contract with NASA for 12 flights of its Falcon 9 rocket and Dragon spacecraft to the International Space Station, replacing the Space Shuttle after its retirement in 2011. Initially, the Falcon 9 and Dragon will replace the Shuttle's cargo-carrying function, while the personnel-carrying function will be performed by the Soyuz. However, SpaceX has designed the Falcon 9/Dragon for astronaut transport, and the Augustine Commission has recommended that astronaut transport be handled by commercial companies such as SpaceX.

Musk sees space exploration as an important step in the expansion - even preservation - of human consciousness. Musk has said that life on multiple planets can serve as a defense against threats to the survival of the human species.

Musk's goal is to reduce the cost of manned space travel by a factor of 100. He founded SpaceX with $100 million of his previously accumulated fortune and remains the CEO and CTO of his Hawthorne, California-based company.

In seven years, SpaceX designed the Falcon family of rockets and Dragon multipurpose spacecraft from the ground up. In September 2009, Falcon 1 became the first privately funded liquid-fueled vehicle to put a satellite into Earth orbit. NASA selected SpaceX to be part of the first program that would hand over responsibility for delivering cargo to the International Space Station to private companies. This contract, which has a minimum value of $1600 million and a maximum value of $3.1 billion, has become a cornerstone of the space station. In addition to these services, SpaceX's goals include reducing orbital flight costs and increasing its reliability, both by a factor of ten, while creating the first reusable orbital launch vehicle. In the coming years, Musk will focus on taking astronauts to the International Space Station, and even to Mars.

Starlink

Starlink is SpaceX's project to create a constellation of internet satellites with the goal of providing low-cost broadband, low-latency internet service and global coverage. In 2017, regulatory requirements were completed to launch 11,943 satellites by the mid-2020s.SpaceX also plans to sell satellites for military, scientific and exploration use. In November 2018, the company received authorization from the US government body (FCC) to deploy 7518 broadband satellites, which would be in addition to the 4425 approved in March of the same year.Development began in 2015, and the first satellite prototypes were launched on February 22, 2018. The launch of the first 60 satellites took place on May 23, 2019, and the start of commercial operations of the constellation is expected to begin in 2020.Research and development for the project takes place at SpaceX's facility located in Redmond, Washington.Internet traffic over a geostationary satellite has a minimum theoretical latency of at least 477 ms from the user to the satellite but, in practice, this latency is 600 ms or more. StarLink satellites would orbit between 1/30th and 1/105th of the distance of geostationary orbits and would therefore offer latencies of between 7 and 30 ms, comparable to or lower than existing cable or fiber networks.In May 2018, SpaceX estimated that the total cost of developing and building the constellation will approach USD 10 billion.

Tesla

In 2003 JB Straubel and Elon Musk visited *AC Propulsion*, which had a prototype electric sports car based on a kit of a gasoline car to which they had adapted an electric motor and lithium-ion batteries. The prototype accelerated from 0 to 100 km/h in less than 4 seconds and had a range of 300 kilometers. For months Elon Musk tried to convince them to market the vehicle, but they were not interested in doing so. The members of *AC Propulsion* put him in touch with Martin Eberhard, Marc Tarpenning and founded Tesla Motors with the intention of manufacturing an electric sports car.

In April 2004 Elon Musk decided to invest $6.3 million in Tesla Motors. He was not the only investor, but contributed 98 % of the funding. Other investors included Eberhard and small venture capital firms. Musk continued to invest in all subsequent rounds. As a result of the 2008 financial crisis and forced retirements at Tesla, Musk agreed to take the CEO position in 2008.

Elon designed the logos and lettering for Tesla and SpaceX.

They underestimated the capital needed to create a car manufacturing company. They planned to spend 25 million USD before the first delivery and ended up spending 140 million USD.they bought Lotus Elise bodies to which they installed batteries, electric motor and controllers increasing the weight by more than 60% thus invalidating the original crash tests. In the end the Tesla Roadster had only 7% of common parts with the Lotus Elise.

The assembly of the components was done in a facility rented to them by a Ford dealer.

Elon repeatedly stated that Martin Eberhard is the worst person he has ever worked with. Financial difficulties nearly bankrupted Tesla. By June 2012, 2100 Tesla Roadsters had been sold in 31 countries. The two-seater Tesla Roadster sports car cost about $100,000.

The *Tesla* name was a trademark registered by a private individual in 1995 and Marc Tappening managed to negotiate its purchase for $75,000 USD.

In February 2016, after ten years in the endeavor, they bought the *tesla.com* domain for USD 10 million from Stu Grossman, who was not using it to host websites.

From Tesla's early days Elon recalled:

Learning from the mistakes made with the Roadster, they designed from scratch a 5-door luxury electric passenger car with sports car features. It had telematics software upgrades and could make trips charging at Tesla's network of fast chargers, *superchargers*.

In October 2010 Tesla bought the old NUMMI factory, which had manufactured for GM and Toyota, from which they could hardly use machines or tools and most of it went to scrap.

Automotive component suppliers were reluctant to sell them quality parts and Tesla was forced to manufacture them through vertical integration to avoid disappearing.

On June 22, 2012, production of the 5-seater plus two child seats Tesla Model S electric liftback began. In 2020 the Tesla Model S P100D *Ludicrous* was on sale with acceleration from 0 to 100 km/h in 2.3 seconds, making it the world's fastest accelerating production car.

The Tesla Model X is an electric SUV manufactured by Tesla Motors based on the platform of the Model S. The rear gullwing doors are hinged and open upward.

It began deliveries to the U.S. market in September 2015.In July 2016 Musk released the second part of Tesla's master plan.

In July 2016, Tesla began developing its Autopilot hardware and software in-house, ending its collaboration with *Mobileye*.In November 2016, *SolarCity* was acquired by Tesla, Inc.

The Tesla Model 3 is an electric vehicle that was announced with a base price of $35 000. Its production started in mid-2017. In 2018, 2019 and 2020 it was the best-selling electric model in the world. In 2019 the Tesla Model 3 was the seventh best-selling passenger car in the United States with 154 836 units.

In January 2019 Musk traveled to China for the groundbreaking of Gigafactory Shanghai, which was Tesla's first major plant outside the U.S. The time between groundbreaking and production of the first cars was less than a year.

The Tesla Model Y is an electric *crossover* that shares 75% of the parts with the Tesla Model 3. Deliveries began in March 2020.

By 2020 Tesla had sold one million vehicles cumulatively of its Roadster, Model S, Model X and Model 3 models and imminent production of the Tesla Semi, 2020 Tesla Roadster and Tesla Cybertruck had been announced.

All Tesla vehicles manufactured since 2014 have electronic components for the operation of *Autopilot* (driving assistance) as standard, and since April 2019, all Tesla vehicles have the basic functions of the system activated. Advanced autonomous driving functions (*Full Self-Driving Capabilities*) are optional. *Autopilot* capabilities are updated telematically without taking the cars to the workshop. The *Autopilot* system trains a deep learning neural network with data it collects from the entire fleet of Tesla vehicles equipped with *Autopilot* hardware, which by March 2020 already numbered 950 000. This made Tesla the company that had collected the most actual data for autonomous driving in all kinds of situations.

In early 2020 Tesla became the second largest car manufacturer in market capitalization after Toyota.

In January 2016 Musk held 28.9 million Tesla shares, which was equivalent to 22% of the company.

SolarCity

SolarCity is a photovoltaic products and services company founded in 2006, where his cousin, Lyndon Rive, is the CEO and co-founder. Elon Musk is the principal investor and chairman of SolarCity's board of directors. The idea for the project came about when Musk participated in the 2004 Burning Man festival.

Elon Musk does not run the company's day-to-day operations. In 2011 SolarCity was the largest provider of solar energy systems in the United States. Its goal is to spread solar energy and make it as affordable as possible. The underlying motivation for founding SolarCity and Tesla Motors is to combat global warming. In 2016 SolarCity merged with Tesla, Inc.

Halcyon Molecular

He is a member of the board of directors, along with fellow PayPal founders Luke Nosek and Peter Thiel. Halcyon Molecular was founded with the goal of researching drugs, extending longevity.

Tesla Energy

On April 30, 2015 Tesla introduced two energy storage systems: Powerwall and Powerpack. The Tesla Powerwall is a lithium-ion battery pack used as a backup to a home's electrical grid that can store electrical energy from renewable energy generation, such as solar or wind installations, or store electricity at night when electricity is cheaper. It can be installed outdoors or indoors and does not require an enclosed room, and can also be installed in remote locations without access to the grid.

Neuralink

Neuralink is a nanobiotechnology company founded by Musk that aims to integrate the human brain with artificial intelligence. The company was founded in 2016 and first became known to the general public in March 2017. The company focuses on creating devices that can be implanted into the human brain, with the ultimate purpose of helping humans merge with software and keep pace with advances in artificial intelligence. These enhancements could improve memory or enable more direct interaction with computing devices.

OpenAI

OpenAI is a non-profit artificial intelligence (AI) research company that aims to promote and develop friendly artificial intelligence in a way that benefits humanity as a whole.

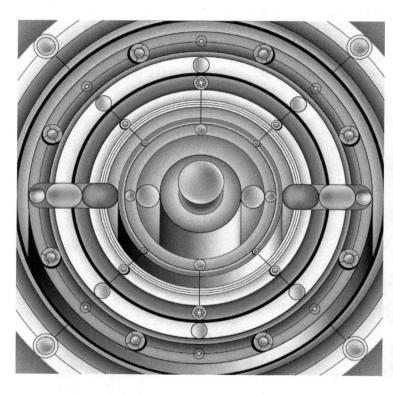

The Boring Company

The Boring Company is an excavation and infrastructure
company founded by Elon Musk in late 2016, after first
mentioning the idea on his Twitter account. Musk claimed
that difficulty with Los Angeles traffic and the limitations of
a 2D transportation network were the inspiration for the
project.In February 2017, the company began by digging a
9-meter wide, 15-meter long, 4.5-meter deep test trench at
the SpaceX offices in Los Angeles, due to the fact that
construction there does not require permits. In early 2018
the Boring Company was spun off from SpaceX forming a
separate company. Ninety percent of the shares went to
Elon Musk and 10 percent to early employees. In
December 2018, 6 % of the shares were reallocated to
SpaceX.

The company's goal is to improve the method and speed
of excavation sufficiently to establish a subway tunnel
network that is economically feasible.

At the end of April 2017, the company started using a
tunnel boring machine to begin construction of a usable
tunnel at SpaceX, as Musk had announced in March of the
same year. In May 2019 the company won a USD 48.7
million project to transport people under Las Vegas. In
September they began preparations and construction in
October 2019. On November 15, 2019 they began
tunneling the first tunnel and completed it on December
27, 2019. Musk announced that it would be operational in
2020.

Method of work

He uses his version of the scientific method:

1. A question is asked.
2. Gather all possible evidence on the matter.
3. It develops axioms based on evidence and attempts to assign a probability of truth to each.
4. Draw a conclusion based on the evidence to determine: Are these axioms correct? Are they relevant? Do they necessarily lead to this conclusion? How likely?
5. Try to falsify the conclusion. Look for refutations from others to help you break your conclusion.
6. If no one can invalidate your conclusion, then you are probably right, but not absolutely right.

Hydrogen

To power an electric car there were two viable options: batteries or a hydrogen-powered fuel cell.

Hydrogen fuel cell cars started to be sold commercially in 2013. In 2017 they sold 6475 units worldwide.In 2019 global sales reached 7574 units of the three available models: Hyundai Nexo, Toyota Mirai and Honda Clarity.However, in 2019 globally 2.2 million battery-powered vehicles were sold, of which Tesla sold 367 820 units.

Autonomous driving

A lidar (acronym LIDAR, *Light Detection and Ranging or Laser Imaging Detection and Ranging*) is a device that allows determining the distance from a laser emitter to an object or surface using a pulsed laser beam. The distance to the object is determined by measuring the time delay between the emission of the pulse and its detection through the reflected signal. In 2019 a car LIDAR was selling for about USD 75 000.

In 2019 in the development of techniques for autonomous driving most companies (Alphabet's Waymo, Ford, Uber, and GM Cruise) used LIDAR while Tesla bet on solving the problem without LIDAR and using a computer processing camera images to recognize and understand the world.

In 2019 Tesla developed and produced its own FSD computer for autonomous driving that processed 2300 fps (frames per second) while consuming only 72 watts.Elon Musk said high-precision GPS maps for autonomous driving were a very bad idea because they led to the system becoming extremely fragile by relying too much on them and not being able to adapt.

In April 2019 Tesla had 425,000 vehicles equipped with hardware for autonomous driving. By March 2020 there were already 950 000 cars that when driving provided Tesla with real (not simulated) driving data that fed its deep learning neural network for autonomous driving.

Philanthropy

Musk is chairman of the Musk Foundation, which focuses its philanthropic efforts on science education, pediatric health and clean energy.

He is a trustee of the X Prize Foundation, which promotes the use of clean energy, serves on the board of directors of the Space Foundation, the *National Academy of Aeronautics and Space Engineering*, the Planetary Society, and the *Space Engineering Advisory Board* of Stanford University.

Musk also serves on the board of trustees of the California Institute of Technology (Caltech).

In 2010, Musk initiated a multi-million dollar program through his foundation to donate solar power systems for critical needs in disaster areas, giving preference to areas where SolarCity does not operate and has no intention of establishing operations. The reason he chose these areas was to make it clear that this was a strictly philanthropic, not-for-profit venture.

The first of this equipment to be used was at a hurricane response center in Alabama that had not received state or federal aid.In July 2011, the Musk Foundation donated $250,000 for a photovoltaic power project in Sōma, Fukushima, Japan, which had been devastated by a recent tsunami.

In 2001, Musk had plans to pursue the "Oasis on Mars" project, which would take a miniature experimental greenhouse to Mars, containing edible plants that would grow in the Martian regolith. However, he decided to postpone the project indefinitely as he came to the conclusion that the fundamental problem preventing humanity from becoming a spacefaring civilization is the lack of development in rocket technology. He decided to address this problem by founding SpaceX in order to create new interplanetary rockets.

He is one of the signatories of The Giving Pledge made up of millionaires who make a moral commitment to donate part of their fortune.

In July 2014, comic book artist Matthew Inman and Nikola Tesla's great-grandson, William Terbo, asked Elon Musk to donate $8 million toward the construction of the Tesla Science Center at Wardenclyffe. Musk donated $1 million toward the project and agreed to install a *Tesla Supercharger* in the museum's parking lot.

In January 2015 Musk donated $10 million for the Future of Life Institute to make a global research program to keep artificial intelligence beneficial to humanity.

In October 2018, in an effort to help solve the lead poisoning water crisis in Flint, Michigan, Musk and the Musk Foundation donated $480,000 to install new fountains with filtration systems so that all Flint schools could have safe drinking water. By October 2019, they had ensured that 30,000 children in the 12 school zones had safe drinking water.

Musk is a major donor to the *American Civil Liberties Union* ACLU.

In October 2019 Musk donated $1 million to the 20 million tree planting initiative '#TeamTrees' led by members of the YouTube community and in partnership with the Arbor Day Foundation.

Despite what has been said, philanthropic attitudes have to be put on trial. On the 24th and 25th of 2020, Musk published a series of tweets regarding the 2019 Political Crisis in Bolivia in Bolivia, in which he stated about the Lithium deposits found in that country, saying "We will give a coup d'état to whomever we want."

Awards and recognitions

In 2006, Mikhail Gorbachev presented him with a product design award for Tesla Roadster on behalf of Global Green. In 2007, the Index Design Award honored him for the same model. That year, *R&D Magazine* named Musk Innovator of the Year for SpaceX, Tesla and SolarCity.

Inc Magazine presented him with the Entrepreneur of the Year award in 2007 for his work at Tesla and SpaceX. He also received the George Low Award from the American Institute of Aeronautics and Astronautics for his outstanding contribution to aerospace transportation in 2008. Musk was recognized for his design of the Falcon 1, the first private liquid-fueled vehicle to reach Earth orbit. He received the Von Braun Trophy from the National Space Society in 2008/2009 for his leadership in a significant achievement in space.

He was named to *Time* magazine's 2010 list of the 100 most influential people in the world. *Esquire* magazine named him one of the 75 most influential people of the 21st century. In 2010, he was named the world's Automotive Executive of the Year for demonstrating technological leadership and innovation with Tesla Motors. Musk is the youngest man ever to receive this award. In a 2010 Space Foundation survey, Musk ranked No. 10 (tied with rocketry pioneer Wernher von Braun) among the most popular space heroes. He was recognized as a *Living Legend of Aviation* that same year by the Kitty Hawk Foundation for creating the successor to the Space Shuttle (F9/Dragon).

In June 2011, Musk received for the Heinlein Award for Advances in Space Commercialization. In February of that year, *Forbes* magazine included Musk on its list of the "20 Most Powerful CEOs Under 40 in the United States."

The Federation Aeronautique Internationale, the organization in charge of flight records, awarded Musk the institution's highest honor, the *FAI Gold Space Medal*, for designing the first privately funded rocket to reach orbit. Other recipients of the award include Neil Armstrong, Burt Rutan of Scaled Composites and John Glenn.

He received the *National Conservation Achievement Award* from the National Wildlife Federation for Tesla Motors and SolarCity.

It was honored at Aviation Week 2008 for having the most significant worldwide achievement in the space industry.

In June 2016, *Business Insider* named Musk as one of the "Top 10 Business Visionaries Creating Value for the World," along with Mark Zuckerberg and Sal Khan. In December of that year Musk ranked 21st on Forbes' list of the world's most powerful people.

Honorary Doctorates

- Honorary Doctorate in Design from the Art Center School of Pasadena.
- Honorary Doctorate (DUniv) in Aerospace Engineering from the University of Surrey.

Television

On January 25, 2015, episode number 12 (564 of the total series) of the 26th season of the animated series The Simpsons was presented, called The Musk Who Fell to Earth, in which Elon Musk was introduced as a guest star, playing himself. In this story, Musk portrays himself as a man who, after lending his ideas to the evolution of the automotive industry (without necessarily alluding to Tesla, Inc.), decides to travel the country aboard a spaceship that lands in the Simpson family's backyard. Quickly, Musk and Homer become friends because some of the latter's reflections stimulate new ideas in the young inventor. Homer takes him to the Springfield nuclear plant where Elon quickly displaces Montgomery Burns from his position, causing the plant to be closed and generating discontent in society.

After the broadcast of this chapter, Musk was dissatisfied with an expression at the end of it, where Lisa expresses after his departure that "For a man who likes electric cars, his ship burned a lot of fuel". Such joke received the response of Elon who expressed that:

Interests

He has read many, many books, including Nietzsche, Schopenhauer and The *Hitchhiker's Guide to the Galaxy*. Musk has described himself as a workaholic who spends typically 80 to 100 hours a week on his work at Tesla and SpaceX. On average he sleeps between 6 hours and 6.5 hours a day. On the rare occasions when he has free time, he spends it playing with his children. He has twins and triplets who are two years apart.

Policy

Politically, Musk has described himself as half Democrat and half Republican.

In 2018 he claimed he was not a conservative. "I'm registered as an independent voter and I'm politically moderate. "Due to the rise of automation and artificial intelligence, Musk supports universal basic income.He also supports direct democracy.He has described himself as a socialist.

Musk has said that the United States is the best country that has ever existed on Earth, that democracy would not exist if it were not for the United States, as it prevented its demise in the two world wars and the cold war. He also stated that it would be a mistake to say that the United States is perfect, because it is not, and that the United States has done bad and stupid things.

After Trump's inauguration, Musk agreed to serve on advisory boards for Trump.

In June 2017 and in protest of Trump's decision to withdraw the United States from the Paris climate change agreement, Musk resigned from his advisory councils, saying, "Climate change is real. Leaving Paris is not good for America or the world."

In August 2019 Musk endorsed on Twitter presidential candidate, in the Democratic primary for the nomination, Andrew Yang, whose agenda revolved around the problem of job displacement by automation and artificial intelligence. Musk said in a tweet that universal basic income is "obviously needed."

Pressure groups

In an interview Musk said that he was a significant donor to the Democratic party, but that he also donated quite a bit to the Republican party. He also stated that donations to political parties were a requirement to have a voice to speak to the U.S. government.

A 2012 report by the Sunlight Foundation, an independent foundation that investigates government spending, found that since 2002 SpaceX had spent more than $4 million on US congressional lobbyists and more than $800,000 in contributions to Democrats and Republicans. SpaceX's campaign to gain political support was systematic and sophisticated, and unlike most *startups* SpaceX has maintained a significant lobbying presence in Washington from day one and Musk donated some $725,000 to various campaigns since 2002.

In 2004, he contributed $2,000 to George W. Bush's re-election campaign, $100,000 to Barack Obama's re-election campaign and donated $5,000 to Republican Senator Marco Rubio, who represents Florida, a critical state for the space industry. Together, Musk and SpaceX donated some $250,000 in the 2012 election cycle.

In addition SpaceX hired former Republican Senate Majority Leader Trent Lott to represent the company through the lobbying group Patton Boggs LLP. In addition SpaceX employs other *lobbying* groups.

Religion

Asked if he believed in some kind of destiny, other than physics, in humanity's transition to be a multi-planetary species, Musk responded:

Life as simulation

As a possible solution to the Fermi paradox asking where the aliens are, Musk has considered the simulation hypothesis.

Automobiles

In 1994 he bought an old 1978 BMW 320i for $1400 that he fixed himself. He had it for about two years until he had an accident when a wheel came off when it was being driven by a Zip2 employee and when he worked at Zip2 he bought a 1967 Jaguar E-Type.

In 1999, after selling Zip2, Elon bought a $1 million McLaren F1 that he used every day. While Elon was driving Peter Thiel asked him what the car could do. Musk said "watch this!" as he accelerated and changed lanes. As the car had no traction control it initiated a spin that invaded the oncoming lanes, flew off the roadway to land shattering the body, suspension and glass. Musk got out of the car laughing and Thiel asked him what he was laughing about. Musk told him, "You don't know best. The car is not insured. "The McLaren F1 featured a 6.1-liter, 627-horsepower, 6.1-liter V-12 engine and had carbon fiber bodywork. Only 64 units were produced. Fortunately Elon and his companion, Peter Thiel, co-founder of PayPal, were unharmed. After repairing the McLaren F1, he later sold it for cash. The McLaren F1 was capable of reaching 100 km/h in 3.2 seconds. At the unveiling of the

Tesla Model S P85D Elon said he had matched the 0-60 mph mark in 3.2 seconds of the McLaren F1. In 2016 the Tesla Model S P100D managed to break that mark and set it at 2.28 seconds, making it the world's fastest accelerating production car.

In June 2019, Musk hinted that an amphibious vehicle design based on Wet Nellie's design for the underwater car in the James Bond film *The Spy Who Loved Me* (1977) might be possible. Musk bought Wet Nellie's car in 2013 at a Sotheby's auction for nearly $1 million and in 2019 displayed it at the unveiling of the Tesla Cybertruck.

He also had an Audi Q7 that he didn't like the access to the third row of seats. That was a spur to design the gull-wing doors of the Tesla Model X.

In 2007 I had a Hamann BMW M5.

In 2012 he owned a Porsche 911.

In 2017 a friend gave him a Ford Model T as a gift.

In 2018 he launched his Tesla Roadster into space on a SpaceX Falcon Heavy rocket and will spend millions of years orbiting the Sun.

It also has a Tesla Model S, Tesla Model X and Tesla Model 3 Performance.

Cinema

In 2010 the SpaceX factory was used for the filming of *Iron Man 2* and Musk makes a cameo in the movie.

In 2013 he has a cameo in *Machete Kills*, and the SpaceX facility appears.

In 2014 he appeared in the science fiction film *Transcendence*.

In 2015 he voices his character in *The Simpsons* episode entitled *The Musk Who Fell to Earth* in which Elon Musk goes to Springfield and Homer suggests an idea that could revolutionize the city, but in the end ends up costing Mr. Burns a fortune.

In 2015 he has a cameo in the series *The Big Bang Theory*, in episode 9 of the ninth season, *The Platonic Permutation*, playing himself.

In 2016 he appears as himself in the film *Why Him?* starring James Franco and Bryan Cranston, in which he attends a party that takes place in the film.

In 2014 he appears in the series South Park in the episode Handicar only as a reference. But already later in 2016 he appears in the episodes "Members only", "Not funny" and "The end of the seriesalizacion as we know it" playing himself.

In 2017 he has a cameo in the series *Young Sheldon*, in episode 6 of the first season, *A Patch, a Modem and a Zantac*, as himself.

In 2019, he appears in episode 3 of *Rick & Morty's* fourth season "One Crew Over the Crewcoo's Morty," playing a version of himself from an alternate universe where humans have big fangs named *Elon Tusk*.

Hyperloop

On August 12, 2013 he proposed the *Hyperloop* system as a system that would allow people to be transported between San Francisco and Los Angeles in 35 minutes. Currently the 563 kilometers can be traveled by car in about 5.5 hours on existing roads.

Hyperloop is a new mode of transportation that seeks to change the current paradigm by being fast and cheap for people and goods. Hyperloop is an open design concept, similar to GNU/Linux, in which community input can advance the design and make it a reality. It is a fast, cheap, environmentally sustainable system, with almost immediate departures for the traveler.

It consists of a tube containing low-pressure air through which capsules circulate on an air cushion. The nose of the capsule contains an electric compressor that transfers high air pressure from the nose to the tail of the capsule. The compressor provides levitation and to a lesser degree propulsion.

The project between San Francisco and Los Angeles with two tubes is covered by solar panels on the roof that would generate more than the energy it needs to operate. The solar panels would be 4.25 m wide and cover a distance of 563 km. With a solar energy output of 120 W/m² the system would be expected to produce a maximum peak solar output of 285MW.

The overall system would consume an average of 21MW. This includes the energy needed for propulsion, aerodynamic drag, battery recharging and vacuum pumps. The solar panels would provide an average of 57MW, which is more than enough to operate the *Hyperloop*.

The total cost would be USD 6 billion for the single version and USD 7.5 billion for the large car-carrying version. Amortizing this capital over twenty years and adding operating costs, each single ticket would cost about $20.

The single version of *Hyperloop* would cost 9% of what the high-speed train between Los Angeles and San Francisco would cost.

In January 2015 Elon Musk announced that a *Hyperloop* test track would be built in Texas for companies and students to test their designs.

Music

On March 30, 2019, Musk released a *rap* single to the music platform SoundCloud under the username "*Emo G Records*". Titled "*RIP Harambe*", the song was performed by Yung Jake, written by Yung Jake and Caroline Polachek, and produced by BloodPop. Within ten days, the song had garnered over 2 000 000 plays. On January 30, 2020, Musk released a second song to his SoundCloud profile titled "*Don't Doubt Ur Vibe*".

Musk is believed to be a fan of South Korean girlgroup Loona. This, after Grimes, his current partner and who has collaborated with this group before, posted on the social network Twitter how was his experience in the studio with the girls.

Elon, within a month, responded with a tweet with the word "Loona," stylized in all caps and with lightning bolt emoticons on the ends. Loona fans enthusiastically received Musk's growing interest in this K-Pop group.

In addition, it has been confirmed that Go Won, the eleventh member of Loona, would, according to Grimes, be the godmother of the latter's and Elon's son, X Æ A-Xii Musk.

Tributes on your products

Tesla vehicles include *Easter Eggs*: hidden or undocumented features or functions included as jokes in a computer program.

Musk christened the top acceleration mode of the Tesla Model S as *Ludicrous* and the later level as *Plaid*, copying the speeds of spaceships (*Ludicrous Speed, Plaid Speed*) in Mel Brooks' satirical comedy Spaceballs (1987).*Ludicrous Speed* would be a speed higher than the speed of light in which the visible stars leave a linear trace, while *Plaid Speed* would be an even higher speed in which the stars would leave longitudinal and transverse traces creating a *plaid* pattern of crossed lists like in a Scottish *kilt.*

On Tesla's with *Ludicrous* if you press the *Ludicrous* button and hold it for 3 seconds, the screen changes and represents what it would be like to go in space at faster than the speed of light. It is a reference to the movie Spaceballs.

The sound volume of the Tesla Model S and X goes up to level 11 in homage to a sequence from the mockumentary film *This is Spinal Tap* (1984) directed by Rob Reiner. In the film a musician shows his amplifier in which all the dials go up to 11.

Tesla's *Tesla Emissions Testing Mode* produces fart sounds in either seat and can be programmed to produce them when the turn signal is activated.

SpaceX's first Dragon launch sent as *secret cargo* a cheese in homage to Monty Python.

On Tesla's if the vehicle name is changed to *Patsy, Rabbit of Caerbannog, Mr. Creosote, Biggus Dickus* or *Unladen Swallow the* foot of Cupid appears and a fart sounds in reference to *Monty Python.*

Since October 2018 all Tesla vehicles incorporate the old Atari games *Missile Command, Asteroids, Lunar Lander* and *Centipede.*

Since September 2018 Teslas with Autopilot can select *Mad Max Mode* as the most aggressive mode for automated lane changes. It is a tribute to the movie *Mad Max* (1979) directed by George Miller.

For the Tesla Model 3, he designed a sophisticated reservoir for the cooling system called Superbottle, which is printed with a superhero-style drawing of a caped bottle.

In Tesla vehicles when *Sentry Mode* is activated, the image of the HAL 9000 computer from Stanley Kubrick's 2001 A Space Odyssey appears. It can be activated with the voice command *Keep Summer Safe in* reference to Rick and Morty season 2 episode 6, in which Rick orders his vehicle to protect Summer (Morty's sister), who stays inside the vehicle.

In Tesla cars when the name of the vehicle is changed to "42" the message "Life, the Universe and Everything" appears. In Douglas Adams' book *Hitchhiker's Guide to the Galaxy*, the supercomputer *Deep Thought* is asked what the meaning of life is and after 7.5 million years it answers: "42".

On Tesla vehicles with air suspension, after pressing the T logo and typing the code 007, the amphibious Lotus Esprit that appeared in the 1977 James Bond film *The Spy Who Loved Me* comes out.

In Tesla cars activating the Autopilot lever 4 times shows the road with rainbow colors. This is a reference to the game *Mario Kart* for Nintendo 64.

When a Tesla car has the battery charged for a range of 121 km and the phone's APP is opened, multiple references to the 1985 movie *Back to the Future* appear.

If you press the Tesla logo for 5 seconds and enter the code "MARS" the navigation screen shows what a vehicle driving on Mars would see.

On a Tesla if you press the phone icon for 3 seconds the text changes to *Ahoy-Today* which was the phrase proposed by the inventor of the telephone Alexander Graham Bell to answer a telephone.

In November 2019 Musk unveiled the Tesla Cybertruck, an electric pickup truck. The presentation was in Los Angeles, the same city, the same month and the same year as the movie *Blade Runner*, which inspired the design of the Cybertruck.

Personal life

In December 2000 he took a vacation in Brazil and a game reserve in South Africa. In January 2001 he returned to California and a few days later began to feel ill. He was initially diagnosed with viral meningitis, which was treated and he was discharged. A few days later he took a turn for the worse and was transferred to Sequoia Hospital in Redwood City. He was diagnosed and treated for malaria. While in the intensive care unit, the strain was found to be *plasmodium falciparum, which is the* most lethal. They changed the treatment to a more aggressive one that could have dangerous side effects such as arrhythmias and organ failure. He almost died, lost 20 kilos and took 6 months to fully recover.

Musk lives in Bel-Air, California. In 2000 Elon married his first wife, Canadian author Justine Wilson, whom he met when they were both students at Queen's University. In 2002 they had a son named Nevada Alexander Musk, who at ten weeks old died of sudden death syndrome. Musk and Wilson have five children: a set of twins and triplets. They separated in 2008.

That same year he met British actress Talulah Riley. They married in 2010 and divorced in 2012. They remarried in 2013 and ended up legally separated. In November 2017 he ended his relationship with actress Amber Heard due to their scheduling conflicts.

On May 7, 2018, Musk began dating Canadian singer Grimes and in January 2020 they announced they were expecting their first child, Musk's sixth. On May 4, 2020, their son, X AE A-XII Musk was born.The couple announced their separation in September 2021.The couple returned in December 2021. In March 2022, it was made public that their second biological daughter with Grimes, whom they named Exa Dark Sideræl, was born via surrogacy in December 2021; their eighth child in total.

In July 2022, *Insider went* public that he had twins with Shivon Zilis, director of operations and special projects at Neuralink, in November 2021.

Kimbal Musk is a director of Tesla, Inc. and SpaceX. He is also Elon's trustee for both companies in the event his brother becomes incapacitated.

While participating in *Saturday Night Live* in May 2021, Musk claimed to have Asperger's syndrome.

Controversies

In October 2008, after Musk confirmed that Tesla Motors was running out of cash, it came to light that he had hired an outside ITC firm to review all of Tesla's emails and instant messages. Subsequently, a forensic investigator took fingerprints from printouts that had been discarded near the photocopier that was used to leak the email. The investigation indicated that the employee responsible for posting the message stating the company's financial status was Peng Zhou. Musk offered Zhou the option to apologize to the company and resign, an option he took to avoid prosecution.

On May 26, 2009, former Tesla Motors CEO Martin Eberhard filed a complaint in San Mateo County, California, against Tesla Motors and Musk for defamation and breach of contract. The case was based on the question of who should be called the true founder of Tesla. On July 29, 2009, a San Mateo County Superior Court judge dismissed Eberhard's request that he be declared one of only two founders of the company. Tesla said in a statement that the ruling was "consistent with Tesla's belief in a team of founders, including current CEO Elon Musk and CTO JB Straubel, who were instrumental in the creation of Tesla from its conception."

In early August, Eberhard dropped the case, and the parties reached a settlement on September 21. Although the terms of the settlement are confidential, it included a provision in which the parties deemed Eberhard, Musk, JB Straubel, Marc Tarpenning and Ian Wright to be the five co-founders of Tesla Motors.

In 2018 Musk announced the creation of a project called "Pravda" (or Pravduh), which in Russian means "Truth" that would evaluate the credibility of the media and fake news. This announcement came after his controversies with different journalists on social networks, specifically after pointing out that the media would be - according to Elon Musk - under pressure from oil companies and automakers through advertising payments.

During a debate on social media, Elon Musk was accused of anti-Semitism by some internet users and journalists after he responded to a message from journalist Joshua Topolsky in which he explained to Elon how "powerful people" controlled the polls, to which Elon Musk responded that the same "powerful people" who controlled the polls also controlled the media. This was misinterpreted by some social media users, personalities and journalists, forcing Elon Musk to give an in-depth explanation of the situation.

SEC

On August 7, 2018 Elon posted the tweets:

The *U.S. Securities and Exchange Commission* (SEC) filed charges against Elon Musk alleging that the potential transaction was unsafe and dependent on numerous contingencies. Musk had not agreed on the details of the deal with potential financial partners, and his claims did not match the facts. The SEC claimed that the misleading tweets sent Tesla's stock up 6% on August 7, causing disruption in the market. On September 29, 2018 Musk and Tesla reached a settlement without admitting or denying the SEC's allegations that required that:

- Elon Musk will step down as Chairman of Tesla to be replaced by an independent for at least 3 years.

- Tesla would appoint two new independent directors to its board.

- Tesla would establish a new committee of independent directors and would monitor and oversee Musk's communications.

- Musk would pay $20 million and Tesla would pay another $20 million. The $40 million would be distributed among the injured shareholders.

On October 4, 2018 Elon wrote the tweet:

This was in reference to stock market attacks by short sellers betting on Tesla's stock plunging in value. On May 21, 2019, 31 % of Tesla's available shares were under short attack.

The short attacks occurred for years and at unprecedented levels in the stock market without the SEC opening an investigation and setting limits.

The SEC took this opportunity to sue him on February 25, 2019 for contempt and breach of the September 2018 agreement as those tweets had not been approved in advance by Tesla's counsel. On April 30, 2019, the judge imposed an amendment to the September 2018 agreement whereby Tesla's counsel would be required to approve in advance all of Elon Musk's public written communications containing information from:

- Tesla's financial condition, statements, results, earnings or governance,

- Potential or proposed mergers, acquisitions, dispositions, tender offers or joint ventures by Tesla.

- Production, sales or delivery numbers (actual or calculated) that would not have been shared, or that differed from Tesla's official direction.

- Proposed lines of business unrelated to Tesla's current ones (defined in the registration as *vehicles, transportation and sustainable energy products*).

- Changes in the status of securities, credit facilities, financing or loan agreements.

- Legal decisions, regulatory recommendations or non-public decisions.

- Anything requiring the filing of an SEC Form 8-K, including changes in control of the company, its officers and directors.

- Any other matter that Tesla or a majority of its independent members within the board believes requires prior approval.

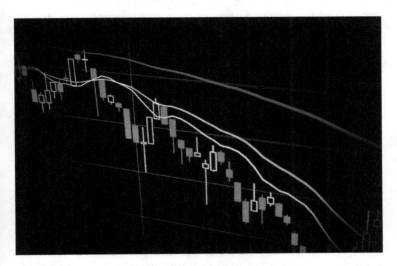

The rescue in the Tham Luang cave

In July 2018 Musk attempted to assist rescuers during the Than Luang cave rescue by directing his employees to manufacture a small rescue capsule with a diameter of 38 cm that would fit a boy. Musk, responding to requests from Twitter users, contacted the Thai government. He organized the work of engineers from his companies to design against the clock a small submarine to aid in the rescue and documented the entire process on Twitter. Richard Stanton, director of the international rescue team also urged Musk to build the mini-submarine as a backup in case the flooding worsened.Engineers from SpaceX and The Boring Company fabricated the mini-submarine in one day from a liquid oxygen transfer tube from a Falcon 9 rocket and flew it to Thailand.They named it "Wild Boar" after the children's soccer team.Its design, based on input from the diving team, was a 150 cm long, 30 cm diameter tube that weighed 41 kg. It was manually propelled by divers and had compartments for attaching diving weights and adjusting buoyancy, with the intention of safely transporting children who might have difficulty learning the diving techniques required to exit the cave without panicking. In case the mini-submarine did not fit into some sections of the cave, Elon Musk asked the Californian inflatable boat company to build inflatable escape pods.When the mini-submarine arrived in Thailand 8 of the 12 boys had already been rescued using anesthesia, diving masks and oxygen.Thai authorities decided not to use the submarine.In March 2019 Elon Musk was awarded the Order of the Direkgunabhorn (*Member of the Order of the Direkgunabhorn*) by the King of Thailand for his and his team's contributions to the rescue mission.

Reactions

The supervisor of the rescue operation, Narongsak Osatanakorn, said the submarine was technologically sophisticated, but did not fit the mission to enter the cave. Vernon Unsworth, an amateur speleologist who had spent six years exploring the cave and who advised on the rescue, criticized on CNN that the submarine was nothing more than a publicity stunt because it had no chance of success and that Musk did not understand what the cave's passages were like. And that furthermore.

Musk claimed on Twitter that the device would have worked and referred to Vemon Unsworth as a "pedo guy," which caused backlash against Musk. Musk deleted the tweets. He also deleted a tweet in which he told a critic of the device.

On July 16, 2018 Unsworth stated that he was considering legal action against Musk's comments.Two days later Musk apologized for his comments.On August 28, 2018 in response to a criticism from Twitter, Musk wrote the tweet:

The next day a letter from attorney Lin Wood dated August 6 was made public showing that he was preparing a defamation lawsuit.A self-proclaimed private investigator emailed Musk with an offer to dig up dirt on Unsworth's past. Musk accepted the offer in August 2018 and paid him $50,000.It later emerged that the investigator was a felon convicted of fraud offenses.On August 30, using details of the alleged investigation, Musk sent a *BuzzFeed News* reporter, who had written about the controversy, an email headed "Off the record" in which he claimed Unsworth was an:

The latter was denied by Unswoth's partner. On Sept. 5 the reporter tweeted a copy of the email saying the "off the record" was an agreement between two and he had not agreed to it.In mid-September Unsworth filed a lawsuit in federal court in Los Angeles.In his defense Musk argued that in colloquial language "pedo guy" was a common insult in South Africa where it grew up synonymous with "sinister old man" and is used to insult appearance and behavior. The Dictionary of Contemporary Slang defines the term "fart" as.

The defamation case, in which Unsworth was claiming $190 million, began on December 4, 2019 in Los Angeles. During the trial Musk apologized to Unsworth again for the original tweet. On Dec. 6, the jury found Musk not guilty of defamation.

Joe Rogan

On The Joe Rogan Experience podcast show 1169 on September 7, 2018, Elon recommended to Rogan, a fan of fast cars, that he buy a Tesla Model S P100D *Ludicrous*, which he did shortly thereafter. Elon drank whiskey. Rogan invited him to smoke marijuana and Elon took a puff. Recreational marijuana use is legal in California, where the interview took place.Musk posted the tweet:

The interview had a negative impact on his, Tesla's and SpaceX's image.

COVID-19

Musk has spread misinformation about the COVID-19 pandemic, including promoting chloroquine as a treatment for the virus and claiming that death statistics were manipulated by researchers and doctors for financial reasons. At the beginning of the pandemic, he claimed that children are "essentially immune" to the SARS-CoV-2 coronavirus. Musk repeatedly criticized confinements and violated local protocols by reopening a Tesla factory in Fremont, California.In March 2020, commenting on a *New York Times* report that China had reported no new cases of domestic spread of the new coronavirus, Musk predicted that there would be "probably close to zero new cases in the U.S. by the end of April as well."*Politico* later called this statement "one of the boldest, safest, and most spectacularly incorrect predictions [of 2020]." In November 2020, he tweeted misinformation about the effectiveness of COVID-19 testing. In April 2021, he tweeted a modified version of a Ben Garrison comic strip with a cartoon of Bill Gates and an anti-vaccine message.

Dogecoin

By June 2022, Musk was charged with alleged pyramid scheme, in which he promoted information related to buying Dogecoin.

See all our published books here:
https://campsite.bio/unitedlibrary